Hi there!

My name is Daniel Scalosub. Apart from being the founder of MegaGeex, I'm also known as Mia and Gaia's dad :)

I started the company back in 2018 to inspire and influence my 6-year-old twin girls toward believing that they can do ANYTHING they want.

My girls didn't take my word for it. They wanted to see proof!

I set out to find proof in real stories of people that could provide support to my thesis. I noticed that almost all the famous, successful people that we know and love had a few things in common:

1. None of them had it easy. Their road to success was filled with trial and error.
2. They all had unbelievable grit!
3. They turned their failures into stepping stones towards success!

Some of the stories included people like Thomas Edison who invented the light-bulb not before failing over a thousand times. The Wright Brothers, who risked their lives trying to build and fly the first airplane, Marie Curie that was so poor she almost starved and froze while studying, and of course, Albert Einstein who is considered a genius today but couldn't find work as a teacher at first. The list obviously goes on and on. These are the Megageex.

I gathered all these amazing stories and characters and with the help of amazing artists, writers and talented individuals we've developed a range of products that bring together fun activities and fascinating life lessons of the MegaGeex to inspire my twin girls and every other kid out there!

Have fun!

Yours truly,
Daniel Scalosub - Founder
MegaGeex

" Before you act, *listen*.
Before you react, *think*.
Before you spend, *earn*.
Before you criticize, *wait*.
Before you pray, *forgive*.
Before you quit, *try*.

Ernest Hemingway. "

FAIR USE OF THIS PRODUCT

At MegaGeex, we love making content designed to help build better learners, and empower parents and educators alike to give kids hands-on inspiration to grow into the world-changing adults we want them to be. To be able to do that, we need your help to guarantee that we have the resources to continue to create great content.

Our books are for **non-commercial use** only. If you want to use them in a situation where you receive compensation, or want to share with a class or with other families, kindly reach out to us for a **professional license**.

No portion of this book may be reproduced, stored in a retrieval system, or transmitted in any form or by any means, mechanical, electronic, photocopying, recording, or otherwise, without written permission from MegaGeex. You're assisting us by adhering to these rules!

Questions? Feel free to contact us at **hello@megageex.com** and we'll be happy to help. If someone you know would like to use one of our books, or you are interested in further MegaGeex products, our full catalog can be found at **www.megageex.com**.

As always, we thank you for your support, and for granting us the ability to help you build a better future through today's little learners.

Nikola Tesla

Serbian scientist, inventor, and futurist (1856 - 1942). Designed the alternating current (AC) model that provides electricity to homes. Pioneered radio transmissions and wireless technology.

Rosalind Franklin

English chemist (1920 - 1958). Proved the double-helix model of DNA, the building blocks of all life. Her work on the structure of viruses contributed to founding the field of structural virology.

Thomas Edison

American inventor and entrepreneur (1847 - 1931). Considered "America's greatest inventor". Invented the light bulb, the phonograph, the first motion picture camera, early electric power generators, and over a thousand other inventions.

George Washington Carver

American agricultural chemist and agronomist (1860s - 1942). Developed methods for improving soil fertility, and crops versatility. Created products with peanuts, which gave him the nickname "the Peanut Man".

Galileo Galilei

Italian scientist (1564 - 1642). Considered the "father of modern physics". Pioneered the "scientific method" of learning through observation, asking questions and seeking answers by doing experiments.

The Wright Brothers

American aviation pioneers and inventors (Orville 1871 - 1948, Wilbur 1867 - 1912). They invented and built the first motorized airplane and were the first men to fly it in December 1903.

Isaac Newton

English mathematician and scientist (1642 - 1727). Formulated the laws of gravity, motion, and energy. Developed calculus, a new type of math for understanding and describing continuous change.

Madam CJ Walker

American businesswoman, entrepreneur, and social activist (1867 - 1919). Created the first cosmetics and hair care line of products for African-American women. First self-made American female millionaire.

Wolfgang Amadeus Mozart

Austrian composer and child prodigy (1756 - 1791). Considered one of the most popular composers in western history, having composed more than 600 works. His music had a tremendous influence on subsequent western music.

Alexander Graham Bell

Scottish scientist, inventor, and teacher of the deaf (1847 - 1922). Invented the first practical telephone and founded AT&T, the world's first telephone company.

Jane Austen

English writer and author (1775 - 1817) who wrote such classic books as Pride & Prejudice, Emma, and Sense & Sensibility which challenged country life in 1800s century England.

Charles Darwin

English naturalist and biologist (1809 - 1882). Pioneered the science of evolution. His work *On the Origin of Species* shows how beings evolve over time through natural selection.

Ada Lovelace

English mathematician and writer (1815 - 1852). Regarded as the "world's first computer programmer". Wrote the first computer algorithm based on Charles Babbage's Analytical Machine.

Leonardo Da Vinci

Italian inventor, artist, and naturalist (1452 - 1519) whose wide-ranging works include the Mona Lisa, the first helicopter, and is considered one of the most brilliant people to have ever lived.

Alan Turing

English mathematician (1912 - 1954). Considered the "father of computer science" and pioneered artificial intelligence. Built early computers to break German codes and help win World War II.

Marie Curie

Polish physicist and chemist (1867 - 1934). The first woman to win the Nobel Prize for her discovery of radioactivity, and the first person to win the Nobel twice. Discovered the elements radium and polonium.

Albert Einstein

German physicist (1879 - 1955). One of the world's most influential scientists, whose work on light, gravity, time and space changed the way we understand our universe. Formulated the Theory of Relativity and Nobel Prize winner in Physics.

Solution on page 41

1= White　　　2= Black　　　3= Grey　　　4= Skin color　　　5= Yellow

Who am I? _____

" I have been impressed with the urgency of doing.

Knowing is not enough; we must apply.

Being willing is not enough; **we must do**.

Leonardo da Vinci **"**

Leonardo
Da Vinci

Solution on page 41

1= White   2= Black   3= Dark brown   4= Dark skin color   5= Green   6= Orange   7= Red

Who am I? _____

Obstacles don't have to stop you.
If you run into a wall, don't turn
around and give up.
Figure out how to *climb it,*
go through it, or work *around* it.

Michael Jordan

George
Washington
Carver

Solution on page 41

1= White 2= Black 3= Yellow 4= Skin color 5= Blue 6= Brown

Who am I? _____

"

The **more** that *you* read,
the **more** things *you* will know.
The **more** that *you* learn,
the **more** places *you*'ll go.

Dr. Seuss. "

Nikola
Tesla

Solution on page 41

1= White   2= Black   3= Blue   4= Skin color   5= Brown

Who am I? _____

"You're **braver** than you believe, **STRONGER** than you seem, and *smarter* than you think.

A.A. Milne/Christopher Robin "

Alan Turing

Solution on page 41

1= White   2= Black   3= Dark grey   4= Skin color   5= Yellow

Who am I? _____

"All things are **difficult** before they are *EASY*

Thomas Fuller"

Ada Lovelace

Solution on page 41

1= White   2= Black   3= Grey   4= Skin color   5= Yellow   6= Blue

Who am I? _____

"**Success** is not final,
FAILURE is not fatal.
It is the courage
to continue that counts."

Winston Churchil

Charles
Darwin

Solution on page 42

1= White   2= Black   3= Grey   4= Skin color   5= Red   6= Blue

Who am I? _____

19

" *Success* is the ability to go from one failure to another with no loss of ENTHUSIASM. **"**

Winston Churchill

Marie Curie

Solution on page 42

1= White   2= Black   3= Grey   4= Skin color   5= Green   6= orange   7= Purple

Who am I? _____

"

Courage is not the absence of *fear*,

but the TRIUMPH over it.

Nelson Mandela

"

Galileo
Galilei

Solution on page 42

1= White   2= Black   3= Dark skin color   4= Dark brown   5= Red   6= Yellow

Who am I? _____

"Nothing is particularly hard if you **break it down** into small jobs.

Henry Ford "

The Wright Brothers

Solution on page 42

1= White   2= Black   3= Grey   4= Skin color   5= Red   6= Yellow

Who am I? _____

"The important thing is to not stop questioning. CURIOSITY has its own reason for existing."

Albert Einstein

Albert Einstein

Solution on page 42

1= White   2= Black   3= Grey   4= Skin color   5= Purple

Who am I? _____

"What we know is a drop, what we don't know is an **OCEAN.**

Isaac Newton "

Isaac Newton

Solution on page 42

1= White   2= Black   3= Dark grey   4= Skin color   5= Blue   6= Pink

Who am I?_____

"Believe you can and you're halfway there.

T. Roosevelt "

Alexander
Graham Bell

Solution on page 43

1= White   2= Black   3= Grey   4= Skin color   5= Green   6= Red

Who am I? _____

" It is not what we *say* or think that defines us, but what we do.

Jane Austen "

Jane
Austen

Solution on page 43

1= White   2= Black   3= Blue   4= Skin color   5= Red

Who am I? _____

"Perseverance is **failing** 19 times and succeeding the 20th.

Julie Andrews "

Madam C.J. Walker

Solution on page 43

1= White   2= Black   3= Grey   4= Skin color   5= Green   6= Red

Who am I? _____

"You miss 100% of the shots you **don't take.**

Wayne Gretzky. "

Rosalind Franklin

Solution on page 43

1= White   2= Black   3= Yellow   4= Skin color   5= Blue   6= Brown

Who am I? _____

"Why fit in when you were born to STAND OUT?

3" /

Dr. Seuss

Wolfgang
Amadeus
Mozart

Solution on page 43

1= White   2= Black   3= Blue   4= Skin color   5= Dark grey   6= Brown   7= Red

Who am I? _____

"The most certain way to succeed is **always** to try just *one more time*...

Thomas Alva Edison "

Thomas Edison

Page 7

Marie Curie noticed that some elements put off heat. Good thing she did: lots of things in our world run off what she called radiation! Her methods have helped create machines that save millions of lives every day!

Page 9

George Washington Carver wanted all farmers to grow the best crops. He also wanted to keep the land healthy. That is why he supported crops like peanuts that are healthy for soil: that's why they call him "the Peanut Man"!

Page 11

When **Ada Lovelace** was a little girl she became very sick. She could not even leave her bed. To keep her lessons, she studied birds: how did they fly? She built models to try to discover the answer!

Page 13

Alan Turing's work with computers helped create some of the first computers. He thought computers could make every part of our lives easier. His work helped us develop artificial intelligence, which helps run our lives today!

Page 15

Electricity used to run off of direct current—which was very dangerous! **Nikola Tesla** saw a better way. He created alternating current electricity. He gave away the secrets of it for free, so everyone could use it—and we still do!

Page 17

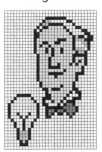

Whenever someone has a good idea, they sometimes say a "lightbulb" has gone off. **Thomas Edison** had tons of great ideas, and he wanted to brighten the world. Now our world is all lit up, because of Edison's good works!

Page 19

Music makes the world go around! **Mozart** could hear a song once and write it down from memory. But he never stopped practicing: he studied music every day, trying to get better! Even today people call him a master!

Page 21

The faster something goes, the more energy it makes: that's what E=mc2 means! **Einstein's** little equation has helped us, from knowing how stars work to changing how we see space and time!

Page 23

Beauty is the eye of the beholder: and **Madam C.J. Walker** had quite an eye! She gave African-American women ways to look beautiful, and it made her America's first African-American female self-made millionaire!

Page 25

Galileo realized his world was not as it seemed. He used telescopes to see things no one had seen before: far planets and distant moons! Though people told him he was wrong and punished him, we know he was right!

Page 27

Before the telephone, it took days or weeks for a letter to arrive from friends and family. **Alexander Graham Bell** changed that: because of his invention, we can see our friends and text them instantly from all over the world!

Page 29

DNA is the building blocks of life. For a long time we did not know what it looked like, but **Rosalind Franklin** changed that with a picture. Now we can fix DNA and change people's lives!

Page 31

Do you have a hobby? **Charles Darwin** did as a kid: collecting bugs! This hobby helped make him famous, and led to his work with evolution. Your hobbies can change the world!

Page 33

Originally the **Wright Brothers** worked on their plane in their garage. They were driven by their passion. Their passion took flight, and now we can fly all over the air and in space! Find your passion!

Page 35

An apple a day won't keep **Isaac Newton** away! Watching an apple fall, he realized that something pulled that apple. He discovered gravity and wrote the Laws of Motion! Who knows what you can see by watching?

Page 37

With her six novels **Jane Austen** transformed English literature by writing about regular people in everyday life. Her stories were often comic but also described moral problems.

Page 39

Considered by many to be the greatest painter of all times, **Leonardo da Vinci's** brush painted 2 of the world's most famous pictures: the Mona Lisa and The Last Supper

Activity books

3D-Diy

Accesories

puzzles

Posters

Tshirts

44

Made in the USA
Monee, IL
03 September 2020